The Home Owner's Handbook to Avoid Foreclosure

10 Solutions for Today's Real Estate Crisis

RUDY LIRA KUSUMA

The Legal Stuff

RUDY LIRA KUSUMA, COLDWELL BANKER New Century, and the publisher have done their best to produce a high quality, helpful and informative book. However, they make no representations or warranties of any kind with regard to the completeness or accuracy of the content of this book. They accept no liability of any kind for any losses or damages caused or alleged to be caused, either directly, or indirectly, from using or acting on any of the information contained in this book. All links are listed for information purposes only, and are not warranted for content, accuracy, or other implied or explicit purposes. All photos and images contained within this book are owned by the author either through purchase or production or used with the express written permission of a 3rd party. If you choose to follow the advice contained in this book, you acknowledge that you are entirely responsible for your own actions and results and that you are using these ideas, tips and suggestions at your own risk.

This book is to be used only for entertainment purposes. The author and publishers do not claim the sufficiency of this book as the sole resource for anyone attempting to perform any other real estate transaction.

This book does not substitute one-on-one personal counseling with a real estate professional. As always, you should seek legal and tax counsel for any matter related to real estate.

FREE Foreclosure Prevention Seminar
Rudy L. Kusuma hosts monthly foreclosure prevention
seminar as part of his community outreach programs.
Most of the live events are hosted in his office in
San Gabriel, California.
Please check the upcoming events online at:
www.TeamNuVisionEvents.com

Rudy Lira Kusuma & Associates, REALTORS®
Department of Real Estate License# 01820322
COLDWELL BANKER New Century
Each office is independently owned and operated
960 East Las Tunas Drive
San Gabriel, California 91776
Office: (626) 789-0159
www.SanGabrielValleyBroker.com

Rudy L. Kusuma, *Certified Distressed Property Expert®*

Contents

Rudy L. Kusuma, *Certified Distressed Property Expert®*

REPORT #1:
The 10 Options to Avoid Foreclosure

The current U.S. housing market and national financial crisis has caused untold stress and heartache for many American families. Foreclosure is one of the most devastating financial challenges that a family can face and one that many times can be avoided. The options available to home owners to avoid foreclosure are many. Following is a brief explanation of these solutions, including their benefits and drawbacks:

Home Owners' Note:

_____

_____

_____

Reinstatement

A reinstatement is the simplest solution for a foreclosure, however it is often the most difficult. The homeowner simply requests the total amount owed to the mortgage company to date and pays it. This solution does not require the lender's approval and will 'reinstate' a mortgage up to the day before the final foreclosure sale.

- <u>Benefit</u>: Does not require the mortgage company or lender's approval.

- <u>Drawback</u>: Requires that a homeowner be able to pay all back payments, fines and fees.

Home Owners' Note:

_____

_____

_____

Rudy L. Kusuma, *Certified Distressed Property Expert®*

Forbearance or Repayment Plan

A forbearance or repayment plan involves the homeowner negotiating with the mortgage company to allow them to repay back payments over a period of time. The homeowner typically makes their current mortgage payment in addition to a portion of the back payments they owe.

- <u>Benefit</u>: Allows the homeowner to make back payments over time.

- <u>Drawback</u>: Requires that a homeowner be in a financial position to pay not only their current mortgage, but also a portion of the back payments owed. Some mortgage companies will require a homeowner to 'qualify' for forbearance.

Home Owners' Note:

_____

_____

_____

Rudy L. Kusuma, *Certified Distressed Property Expert®*

Mortgage Modification

A mortgage modification involves the reduction of one of the following: the interest rate on the loan, the principal balance of the loan, the term of the loan, or any combination of these. These typically result in a lower payment to the homeowner and a more affordable mortgage.

- <u>Benefit</u>: Reduces the payment a homeowner is required to make on a monthly basis and may reduce the principal balance of the loan

- <u>Drawback</u>: Requires that a homeowner 'qualify' for the new payment and will often require full documentation. Lender has to be actively pursuing modifications.

Home Owners' Note:

_____

_____

_____

Rent the Property

A homeowner who has a mortgage payment low enough that market rent will allow it to be paid, is able to convert their property to a rental and use the rental income to pay the mortgage.

- <u>Benefit</u>: Allows homeowner to keep property indefinitely.

- <u>Drawback</u>: The issues that can arise with a rental property are many, and rent often does not cover the full cost of property ownership and maintenance.

Home Owners' Note:

_____

_____

_____

Rudy L. Kusuma, *Certified Distressed Property Expert®*

Deed in Lieu of Foreclosure

Also known as a 'friendly foreclosure', a deed in lieu allows the homeowner to return the property to the lender rather than go through the foreclosure process. Lender approval is required for this option, and the homeowner must also vacate the property.

- <u>Benefit</u>: Many times in a successful deed in lieu, the lender will forego their right to a deficiency judgment.

- <u>Drawback</u>: Requires that a homeowner vacate the property, and a deed in lieu may be reported to credit bureaus as a foreclosure.

Home Owners' Note:

_____

_____

_____

Bankruptcy

Many have considered and marketed bankruptcy as a 'foreclosure solution,' but this is only true in some states and situations. If the homeowner has non-mortgage debts that cause a shortfall of paying their mortgage payments and a personal bankruptcy will eliminate these debts, this may be a viable solution.

- <u>Benefit</u>: Does not require lender approval.

- <u>Drawback</u>: If a homeowner cannot afford their mortgage payment, a bankruptcy will only stall—not stop—the foreclosure process. Bankruptcy can be costly, is damaging to credit scores, and can only be declared once every seven years.

Home Owners' Note:

_____

_____

Rudy L. Kusuma, *Certified Distressed Property Expert®*

Refinance

If a homeowner has sufficient equity in their property and their credit is still in good standing, they may be able to refinance their mortgage.

- <u>Benefit</u>: In some cases, this will lower payments.

- <u>Drawback</u>: In today's market, a refinance will almost always raise mortgage payments, and is an expensive process.

Home Owners' Note:

_____

_____

_____

Rudy L. Kusuma, *Certified Distressed Property Expert®*

Servicemembers Civil Relief Act (military personnel only)

If a member of the military is experiencing financial distress due to deployment, and that person can show that their debt was entered into prior to deployment, they may qualify for relief under the Servicemembers Civil Relief Act. The American Bar Association has a network of attorneys that will work with servicemembers in relation to qualifying for this relief.

- <u>Benefit</u>: If qualified, this will lower payments on all consumer debt in addition to mortgage payments.

- <u>Drawback</u>: Must be active military to qualify.

Home Owners' Note:

_____

_____

_____

Sell the Property

Homeowners with sufficient equity can list their property with a qualified agent that understands the foreclosure process in their area.

- Benefit: Allows homeowner to avoid foreclosure and harvest some of their equity.

- Drawback: In many cases today, homeowners do not have sufficient equity to sell their property without negotiating a short sale (see next solution).

Home Owners' Note:

_____

_____

_____

Short Sale

If a homeowner owes more on their property than it is currently worth, then they can hire a qualified real estate agent to market and sell their property through the negotiation of a short sale with their lender. This typically requires the property to be on the market and the homeowner must have a financial hardship to qualify. Hardship can be simply defined as a material change in the financial stability of the homeowner between the date of the home purchase and the date of the short sale negotiation. Acceptable hardships include but are not limited to: mortgage payment increase, job loss, divorce, excessive debt, forced or unplanned relocation, and more.

- Benefit: A short sale allows the homeowner to avoid foreclosure and salvage some of their credit rating. This also keeps foreclosure off the individual's public record, and in many cases will allow the homeowner to avoid a deficiency judgment. Borrower may qualify for another mortgage in as little as 24 months (as opposed to five years for a foreclosure).

- Drawback: Short sales can be a trying process in which a homeowner is best served by contracting with a qualified real estate agent to guide the way.

Home Owners' Note:

_____

_____

_____

Rudy L. Kusuma, *Certified Distressed Property Expert®*

REPORT #2: Short Sales Explained

A short sale can be an excellent solution for homeowners who need to sell, and who owe more on their homes than they are worth. In the past, it was rare for a bank or lender to accept a short sale. Today, however, due to overwhelming market changes, banks and lenders have become much more negotiable when it comes to these transactions. Recent changes in corporate policy and the Obama administration have also improved the chances of getting a short sale approved.

But to be technical, here's a more official definition:

- A homeowner is 'short' when the amount owed on his/her property is higher than current market value.

Rudy L. Kusuma, *Certified Distressed Property Expert®*

- A short sale occurs when a negotiation is entered into with the homeowner's mortgage company (or companies) to accept less than the full balance of the loan at closing. A buyer closes on the property, and the property is then 'sold short' of the total value of the mortgage.

For homeowners to qualify for a short sale, they must fall into any or all of the following circumstances:

- <u>Financial Hardship</u> – There is a situation causing you to have trouble affording your mortgage.

- <u>Monthly Income Shortfall</u> – In other words: "You have more month than money." A lender will want to see that you cannot afford, or soon will not be able to afford your mortgage.

- <u>Insolvency</u> – The lender will want to see that you do not have significant liquid assets that would allow you to pay down your mortgage.

Rudy L. Kusuma, *Certified Distressed Property Expert®*

Rudy L. Kusuma, *Certified Distressed Property Expert®*

REPORT #3:
A Dignified Alternative to Foreclosure

When a mortgage becomes unaffordable, avoiding foreclosure becomes a primary goal. It is a unique situation that adjusts priorities and changes perspectives. For the millions of homeowners unable to make their mortgage payments today, there are alternatives to foreclosure that can lead to an entirely different, more positive financial outcome.

One of the leading solutions to foreclosure today is a short sale. In a short sale, the lender agrees to accept the sale amount, even if it is less than what is owed on the mortgage. In this report, you'll see how the consequences of foreclosure compare to those of a short sale. As a CDPE designated agent, I have been extensively trained in the alternatives to foreclosure and can help you make an informed decision.

Your Future Loans

My goal is to help you get your life back to normal as quickly as possible, and part of that is your ability to own a home again. Here, a short sale can help. After previous mortgage difficulties, owning a home in the near future will depend on your loan eligibility, which is severely impaired by foreclosure. A successfully negotiated short sale will allow you to be eligible for a Fannie Mae-backed loan in only two years, as opposed to five years after a foreclosure (seven years if the property is not your primary residence).

What would it mean to own a home again in three to five years?

When attempting to acquire a mortgage through another company, your loan application will ask whether you've had a property foreclosure in the last seven years. These applications do not ask about any past short sales, meaning if you have avoided foreclosure through a short sale, your chances of securing a future loan with lower interest rates are substantially better.

Also, you can immediately apply for an FHA (Federal Housing Administration) loan after a successful short sale, assuming you are current on your mortgage payments before the sale. If you aren't current, you will be eligible after just three years. If you want to determine your eligibility for this process, contact me as soon as possible.

Your Future Credit

A short sale may only lower your credit score by as little as 50 points.

When facing the possibility of foreclosure, your credit score is also at stake – something that has become a stronger factor in lenders' decisions to provide loans, low interest rates, credit cards, etc.

A short sale, by itself, can lower your credit score by aslittle as 50 points, as opposed to anywhere from 250 to over 300 points in a foreclosure. In addition, a drop in credit due to a short sale can be recovered as quickly as one year, while a foreclosure will affect your credit for at least three years.

Your credit history, which is also taken into account for loans, does not keep record of past short sales, but a foreclosure will be publicly recorded for at least 10 years.

Your Future Employment
Current and future employers have the legal right to check their employees' credit, and many of them do so regularly. If an employer checks your credit, you want the report as clean as possible. Unlike foreclosure, a short sale is not directly reported on your credit (it will usually say "paid as agreed", "paid as negotiated", or "settled").

If your job requires a security clearance – such as police, military or government work – a foreclosure most often presents an issue. Since short sales are currently not explicitly reported on credit reports, they do not challenge most security clearances.

Your Deficiency Judgment

In most states, lenders have the ability to pursue a deficiency judgment, or the difference between the amount the home sold for and what was owed on the mortgage. In some successful short sales, the lender may surrender this ability. However, if the lender does not give up this right, a short sale will present a much smaller deficiency because they typically sell for much more than a foreclosed property.

Contact me for all the information you'll need to know about deficiencies, including California specific laws.

A short sale offers more than the opportunity to strengthen your future financial stability. It offers peace of mind. The value of this foreclosure alternative is why I have taken the time to understand and master the short sale process.

Rudy L. Kusuma, *Certified Distressed Property Expert®*

You deserve a professional level of guidance in your situation, and I offer extensive knowledge and access to updated information about foreclosure avoidance. As a CDPE-designated agent, I have made a commitment to helping as many homeowners as possible. A short sale could make a huge difference in your financial future, so please contact me right away.

Home Owners' Note:

_____

_____

_____

Place Your Confidence in CDPE

With the right assistance, the stress of facing foreclosure becomes manageable. CDPE-designated agents have received the knowledge and training necessary to assess all possible foreclosure alternatives and pursue homeowners' best options. A CDPE-designated agent attends several days of intensive, thorough training on foreclosure avoidance and how to negotiate short sales efficiently and ethically. The highly regarded CDPE logo means you are working with the most informed, up-to-date resource available.

CERTIFIED DISTRESSED
PROPERTY EXPERT©

Rudy L. Kusuma, *Certified Distressed Property Expert®*

Appendix I:

FREE 1-Hour Foreclosure Prevention Counseling

Please complete this short form (pg 27–29) and email to Rudy@RudyLK.com or fax to 626.371.9208

FIRST NAME: _____

LAST NAME: _____

SUBJECT PROPERTY:

ADDRESS: _____

CITY/STATE/ZIP: _____

MORTGAGE LENDERS INFO:
1ST Lender Name: _____
Interest Rate: _____
Monthly Payment: _____
Loan Balance: _____

2nd Lender Name: _____
Interest Rate: _____
Monthly Payment: _____
Loan Balance: _____

Rudy L. Kusuma, *Certified Distressed Property Expert®*

HELOC: _____

Interest Rate: _____

Monthly Payment: _____

Loan Balance: _____

Approximate Market Value: $ _____

Equity: (if any) $_____

Total Amount Behind
on Mortgage Payments: $_____

Tell us your Hardship
What caused you to get behind?

_____

_____

_____

Have you spoken with your lender
regarding any arrangements?
____ NO
____ YES
If YES, what's the outcome:

_____

Type Employment:
Primary: _____
Spouse: _____

Currently what is your total verifiable
monthly net income? $_____

Rudy L. Kusuma, *Certified Distressed Property Expert®*

What is your total household monthly expense, not including house payment? *(electricity, water, gas, phone, food, cable TV/internet, transportation, insurance, credit cards, child care, medical, etc.)* $ _____

Other Liens: _____

Have you filed bankruptcy since your current mortgage was financed? NO _____ YES _____
Date Discharge: _____

Other than this property, how many other properties do you own? _____

If you belong to a homeowners association, are your HOA dues current?
____ YES
____ NO; Amount behind: $ _____

How much money can you raise in 30 days to bring your mortgage current? $ _____

Please complete this short form (pg 27–29) and email to Rudy@RudyLK.com or fax to 626.371.9208

Rudy L. Kusuma, *Certified Distressed Property Expert®*

IMPORTANT WEB SITES

California Department of Real Estate
www.dre.ca.gov

U.S. Department of Housing and Urban Development
www.hud.gov

The Obama Administration's Making Home Affordable Program
www.MakingHomeAffordable.gov

Home Affordable Foreclosure Alternatives (HAFA) Program
MakingHomeAffordable.gov/hafa.html

SHORT SALE PLATINUM: Free, up-to-date foreclosure prevention resources
www.ShortSalesPlatinum.com

Rudy L. Kusuma, *Certified Distressed Property Expert*®

RECOMMENDED READING

In this powerful and one-of-a-kind guide you'll find:

- **Incredibly simple step-by-step instructions for short selling your home made so clear you could do it without an agent (if you'd prefer that route)**

- Sample distress letters and the financial work sheets that you'll need should you decide to attempt a real estate short sale.

Rudy L. Kusuma, *Certified Distressed Property Expert®*

- **The 8 crucial steps that MUST be taken in order to successfully short sale your home (most failures happen when just a single step gets skipped).**

- Why choosing the wrong buyer can kill your chances of a successful short sale, and how to attract and identify the PERFECT buyer.

- **Exactly what the banks want to see when they receive your short sale proposal and how to deliver it in a way that makes them say "Wow!"**

- How to determine if your real estate agent doesn't have a clue and how to locate the pro that you can take to the bank!

- **The key criteria banks look for when deciding whether to accept or reject your short sale proposal.**

- The method you SHOULD be using to get a proper valuation of your home and why you want to avoid a standard appraisal.

- **The secret technique I and a few other top producers use to sell**

Rudy L. Kusuma, *Certified Distressed Property Expert®*

homes for ABOVE the asking price in ANY market.

- How to get a team of experts to handle the entire process for you at zero cost!

- **The 4-Key Questions ALL asset managers need answers to in order to approve any "short offer" on your home.**

- And a boat load more.

We provide everything you'll ever need from an expert advisor.

- Experience selling homes in difficult market conditions.

- Years of experience negotiating with loss mitigation and asset managers.

- The systems, structure and contacts required to get your real estate short sale approved and closed quickly and with the least amount of hassle.

Available online at www.ShortSalePlatinum.com

Rudy L. Kusuma, *Certified Distressed Property Expert®*

ABOUT RUDY L. KUSUMA

Rudy specializes in representing property owners in the area of Foreclosure Prevention, Pre-Foreclosures Sales, and Short Sales. He has negotiated over $30 million dollars of distressed properties sale in today's real estate market. He has experience in negotiating pre-foreclosure sales, short sales, and general distressed properties sales with lenders nationwide, including: East West Bank, Bank of The West, Bank of America, Wells Fargo, Wachovia, CHASE, America's Servicing Company, Green Tree, etc.

You can see his most recent transactions online at www.RudyHomes.com

Areas of Practice:

He specializes in complex transactions representing property owners in disposition of their real estate, and has significant experience in distressed sales, pre-foreclosure sales and short sales.

Rudy L. Kusuma, *Certified Distressed Property Expert®*

Membership:

* Commercial Real Estate CCIM Institute
* CCIM Greater Los Angeles Chapter
* CRS Southern California Chapter
* California Association of REALTORS®
* National Association of REALTORS®
* Arcadia Association of REALTORS®

Awards and Recognitions:

* 2010 California Association of REALTORS® Education Foundation Grant Recipient

* ZILLOW All-Star Badge Recipient

* 2009 #1 Top Producer Award Recipient

* 2009 Diamond Award Recipient

* 2008 Diamond Award Recipient

* COLDWELL BANKER® New Century Multi-Million Dollar Producer

Rudy L. Kusuma, *Certified Distressed Property Expert®*

Education:

Masters in Commercial Real Estate (MCRE)
Lipsey School of Real Estate

MBA in Marketing
California American University

Bachelor of Science in Mathematics
University of Wisconsin – Madison

Award in General Business Studies
University of California - Los Angeles

Certified Residential Specialist (CRS)
National Association of REALTORS®

Graduate REALTOR® Institute (GRI),
California Association of REALTORS®

Real Estate Masters (R.E. Masters™),
California Association of REALTORS®

Rudy L. Kusuma, *Certified Distressed Property Expert®*

Specialized Training:

REO Default Certified Professional (RDCPro™), Default School

Five Star Short Sale and REO Certified, The Five Star Institute

Certified Distressed Property Expert®(CDPE), The Distressed Property Institute

Certified HAFA Specialist, AssetPlanUSA and the California Association of REALTORS®

Pre-Foreclosure Specialist Certification (PSC), PartnerFirst Nationwide Real Estate Network

Short Sales and Foreclosure Resource (SFR) certification, National Association of REALTORS®

To learn more about Rudy L. Kusuma, please visit his website www.SanGabrielValleyBroker.com

---

NOTES:

Rudy L. Kusuma, *Certified Distressed Property Expert®*

NOTES:

Rudy L. Kusuma, *Certified Distressed Property Expert®*

NOTES:

Rudy L. Kusuma, *Certified Distressed Property Expert®*

NOTES:

NOTES:

NOTES:

Rudy L. Kusuma, *Certified Distressed Property Expert®*

NOTES:

Rudy L. Kusuma, *Certified Distressed Property Expert®*

NOTES:

NOTES:

Rudy L. Kusuma, *Certified Distressed Property Expert®*

NOTES:

Rudy L. Kusuma, *Certified Distressed Property Expert®*

NOTES:

www.ingramcontent.com/pod-product-compliance
Lightning Source LLC
Chambersburg PA
CBHW051254170526
45165CB00004B/1707